Mills & Boon Astral Guides

YOU AND YOUR
LIBRA MAN

James Scott Gunn

ACKNOWLEDGEMENTS

The author wishes to express his appreciation to the following authors for their kindness in allowing him to use extracts from their work.

Astrology by Ronald C. Davidson, ARCO
  PUBLICATIONS

Astrology, The Divine Science by Marcia
  Moore & Mark Douglas, ARCANE
  PUBLICATIONS, USA

First published in Great Britain 1974 by Mills & Boon Limited, 17–19 Foley Street, London W1A 1DR.

ISBN 0 263 71614 7

Made & Printed in Great Britain by
C. Nicholls & Company Ltd.

CONTENTS

PREFACE

Understanding your husband, boyfriend, lover, son or boss is often very difficult. You must have asked yourself hundreds of times; "Why did he do that?". You do something that you think will please him, and are hurt and surprised when he loses his temper and shouts at you.

Astrology has a great deal to offer in helping all of us to understand those with whom we are closely involved. Success or failure may, in the long run, depend on how well we really know each other.

Without delving into the technicalities of Astrology I have tried to render a readable and, I hope, enjoyable account of what makes your man tick.

J.S.G.

INTRODUCTION

Any man-woman relationship is something like a high-wire act; maintaining a balance is essential if the people involved are to live in harmony. Marriage, the ultimate relationship, is like a high-wire act in which the performers wear rose-coloured glasses that distort their vision and confuse their minds. When sanity returns, the couple are confronted with learning to live together – and a very painful process it can often be.

You are two quite separate individuals with varying ambitions, hopes and fears. The success of your relationship depends on two things: understanding each other, and being able to communicate freely and honestly. Without them, your relationship can deteriorate into a perpetual battle for one's individuality. You cannot, either of you, be anything but yourself, and no amount of arguing and fighting is going to change that. Once you accept this, you are well on the way to a successful partnership, a wonderful experience within everyone's grasp, but one which many of us fail to enjoy because understanding one's partner can be difficult.

Your boyfriend, your boss, your lover and even your son can be the cause of unnecessary conflict. A deadly serious Scorpio man is a very different person from a fickle Geminian. A Virgo boss might drive you mad with his obsession for minute details. Capturing your Aquarius boyfriend may be a long-drawn-out process if you don't understand him. Your Pisces son might be content to drift and dream his way through life, which can be very annoying for an ambitious mother. What you must realise is that you cannot change these people, but you can learn to understand them.

Astrology is a complex subject, and trying to avoid the technicalities is like trying to live without breathing. I've taken a minimum of breaths. Nevertheless, some explanation is necessary if this book is going to help you. Many claims are made for Astrology and most of them bring disrepute on a subject that can help all of us to live in greater harmony with those nearest and dearest to us. Astrology is a useful guide, not a prophecy. The degree of success must always lie in the hands of the individual.

Popular Astrology, such as the daily forecasts you read in the newspaper, is based on your sun sign. For example, if you are Aries, the sun was in Aries in your birth chart on the day you were born. This is a very important factor in determining what kind of person you are. However, an even more important factor to take into account is the sign that was on the horizon of your birth chart on the day you were born: We call this the ascendant sign. By combining the two it is possible to arrive at a very good understanding of the characteristics of any individual.

Knowledge of anyone's ascendant can give you a much deeper insight into his character. Perhaps your husband or boyfriend is an Aries and you have read many times that he is impulsive and forceful, and, indeed, he probably is. Yet sometimes he displays streaks of caution when you least expect them. This could be due to an ascendant influence of Cancer or Capricorn. You will often find that as a person grows older he increasingly displays his ascendant characteristics and the influence of his sun sign diminishes. The way your partner acts and thinks can be explained by the tension between his ascendant and sun signs. These two factors combined are the basis of my observations.

Your ascendant sign can only be calculated if you know, as near the hour as possible, the time of your birth. Having ascertained this, you can determine your ascendant sign, or that of anyone else in whom you are interested, by referring to the charts on pages 15–31.

1
LIBRA
MAN
September 24-October 23

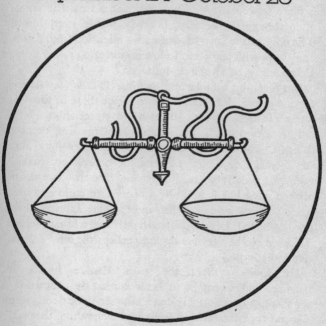

Your Libra man's basic driving force is to seek harmony; harmony in colour and design as well as in his relationships at home, at work, and at play. He yearns to be all things to all men.

Libra babies are charmers and they go on being that way right through life. You may find it difficult to deny him anything, but you should at least try or he may acquire the habit of thinking he just has to smile or weep, if that is more appropriate, and his wish comes true. Librans are often thought to be lazy, but who would exert himself if he only had to snap his fingers for attention from females of all ages who just seem to love ministering to his needs? He's not lazy, he's just over-indulged.

But he is not all take and no give. That is why he is so hard to refuse. A Libran wants to please those he loves and is never loath to show his affection and appreciation.

It is a typically Libran trait to find making decisions difficult. The wise mother should encourage her Libran son to make decisions and fend for himself occasionally, even in his early years. But have a care that you do not ask too much; he is basically a dependent child and needs more positive guidance than most. Some Librans always need to be led. Driving him will only make him miserable. Your son can be very loving and perhaps the most cooperative zodiac type.

His zodiac symbol, the scales, denotes justice and balanced judgements, and he is constantly concerned to see that justice is not only done, but seen to be done. Seeing someone being treated unfairly is the one thing that really annoys him. In other respects he is so attuned to a peaceful life that he will back down from his position nearly every time rather than cause upsets and quarrels.

This lack of firmness may be your Libra man's worst

fault. He finds it very difficult to make clear-cut decisions. An Aries woman, for example, with her super self-confidence, might find that a Libra man drives her to distraction with his dithering over what are, for her, simple, everyday decisions.

Five out of ten henpecked husbands could be Librans. Aries, Leo, Scorpio and Capricorn women will invariably dominate this mild-mannered man. Aries and Leo browbeat him while Scorpio and Capricorn quietly manipulate him like a puppet on a string. He would much rather accede to their demands than risk disharmony. Life is great; why spoil it with too much ambition, too much work, or too much fighting?

An ambitious woman could feel disappointed with a Libra partner. He is probably quite happy to find a job in pleasant surroundings where the pay may not be very good, but the work isn't too arduous either. It can be very frustrating when you are bursting with ideas and the

energy to put them into action, and your partner shows not the slightest inclination to roll up his sleeves to help. He is quite happy to let you have the career for which you have always yearned. Cooperative as ever, he'll stay home and keep house, which he can, in all fairness, do very well. His willingness to work diminishes when his muscles begin to ache and the sweat trickles from his brow. Some Librans can be very lazy.

If you have a Libra boss, the fact that he issues the orders may be due to his ascendant sign characteristics. Generally, a pure Libran would not exert himself to the extent that he would be put at the head of affairs. Such a position means constantly making decisions, which is something he would rather leave to someone else. Nevertheless, you should find this Libra boss reasonably easy to work for. Underlying his ascendant characteristics there will be a willingness to cooperate. He is a peace-loving man and wants everyone on his team to be happy. He cannot tolerate injustice and if it is brought to his notice, you may be in for a shock. A Libra man can hit the roof when the occasion demands.

How you function with him as a team-mate depends on your sun and ascendant signs. If your birth chart is dominated by Aries, then you will be impatient when he takes ages making what seems to you a simple decision. A Virgo influence will incline you towards thinking his working methods are too casual.

Working relationships are much the same as any others in which two or more people are involved. Each person has different values and motivations, and knowing what they are will, in the long run, make for greater harmony. Of one thing you can be sure; a Libra boss will be willing to go more than half way to ensure all round harmony in the office or on the shop floor.

Of all the zodiac types, a Libra man is the most likely to get along with any type of woman. She can nag him, neglect him, love him, or hate him and he will continue to try to improve their relationship, no matter how good or bad it may be.

Your Libra boyfriend is the proverbial lady-killer – good-looking, charming, and able to talk you into anything. A Libra man has a way with women.

If you have plans for leading this boy down the aisle, be prepared for a long struggle. You will first need to vanquish the opposition – and there will be plenty of it, blondes, brunettes and redheads. Most women fall for him because he is so attentive and so eager to please. If you leave him for a moment, he will be surrounded by doting females – and he loves it. Though his intentions towards you are above reproach, a Libra man is easily led away, and then astray.

To add to your troubles Libra people have difficulty in making even the most simple decisions. You may be good-looking, hard-working and adventurous, but so are many other girls. Your Libra boyfriend may be genuinely nonplussed, but pleased, at his popularity. Long engagements are the rule rather than the exception with a Libra boyfriend. Some of them never do take the plunge. However, if you are patient and do finally win him, he will make you a good husband. A Libra man can usually adapt himself to whatever life style his partner wants.

Your Libra partner is never happier than when he is working harmoniously with someone he loves. He will go to great lengths to try to please everybody, which is almost impossible, and inevitably upsets someone, which can bring on moods of despair. Libra is an air sign and, like air, your Libra man's moods can drift unpredictably, driven by the pressure of demands made on him from all sides. Your Libra man valiantly, perhaps foolishly, tries to keep a harmonious balance between warring factions in the family, and among his workmates and friends. Small wonder that occasionally he withdraws from these battles, disillusioned with the selfishness of others less fair-minded than himself.

It is essential to your Libra man's happiness that his home is peaceful and quiet, a place where he can relax in comfort and good taste. A woman who can cope with these basic needs of a Libra partner has a mate who, despite his faults, can be as near to an ideal husband as she is ever likely to find.

2
FINDING YOUR MAN'S ASCENDANT SIGN

To gain a better understanding of what makes your man tick it is necessary to find his ascendant sign. You can do this easily by referring to the charts on pages 18–31. The only thing you need to know is the date and time of his birth. It is very important that you know to the nearest hour when he was born. Having found this, you can consult the charts.

For example, let us assume he was born on September 26 at 4 a.m. Look through the column for September until you come to 4 a.m. You will see that his ascendant sign is Virgo. Or let's say he was born on October 19 at half-past midnight. Look through the October column for 12 p.m. and you will see that his ascendant sign is Leo.

Alongside each ascendant sign you will see a list of your man's good and bad characteristics, and a few suggestions of the qualities he needs to develop to round out his character.

You can now proceed to read in more detail the characteristics he derives from his ascendant sign. By carefully studying these and relating them to Chapter One, Libra Man, you will arrive at a greater understanding of the man in your life.

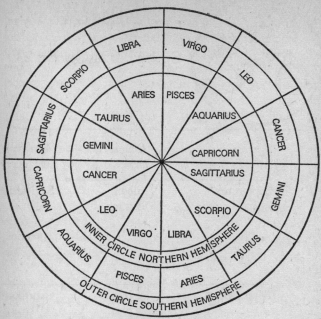

In the southern hemisphere

If you live in the southern hemisphere you need to do a simple calculation to find your ascendant sign. Add twelve hours to the time of your birth. If you were born at 2 a.m., for example, and you add twelve hours, the time is then 2 p.m. Look for 2 p.m. in the ascendant sign charts, and make sure that you are looking at the correct month. Let's suppose that you find the sign is Aquarius. Now refer to the chart on this page. Find Aquarius on the *inner circle*. You will see Leo in the same segment on the *outer circle*. Your ascendant sign is Leo. Similarly, 6 p.m. becomes 6 a.m., and if Aries is on the inner circle, Libra will be your ascendant sign on the outer circle.

LIBRA

September 24-October 23

Month	Hour of birth	Ascendant sign
September	noon 1 p.m.	Sagittarius
September	2 p.m. 3 p.m.	Capricorn
September	4 p.m. 5 p.m.	Aquarius

Nature

Honest, impulsive, jovial, speculative,
optimistic, alert, versatile, *or*
blunt, transparent, flighty, improvident,
over-confident, boisterous, dabbling, superficial
   Must learn to be more: restrained, sincere,
thoughtful of others, purposeful.

Fatherly, just, cautious, economical,
dependable, self-absorbed, practical, *or*
austere, severe, scrupulous, suspicious, mean,
snobbish, morbid, uninspired
   Must learn to: be more sociable, look on the
bright side, cultivate better self-expression.

Intellectual, detached, sctientific,
humanitarian, unconvenional, individualistic,
or
doctrinaire, remote, perverse, incalculable
   Must learn to: have more warmth of feeling,
cultivate the human touch, develop practical
ability.

Month	Hour of birth	Ascendant sign
September	6 p.m.	Pisces
September	7 p.m.	Aries
September	8 p.m. 9 p.m.	Taurus
September	10 p.m. 11 p.m.	Gemini

Nature

Easy-going, imaginative, suggestible, emotional, *or*
lazy, unstable, chaotic, self-pitying
  Must learn to: be more determined, concentrate, avoid alcohol and drugs.

Inspirational, impulsive, assertive, straightforward, sporting, *or*
reckless, aggressive, naive
  Must learn to: show moderation, be more tolerant, be more patient, show more forethought, show more humility.

Conservative, determined, patient, placid, deliberate, *or*
reactionary, obstinate, stolid, lazy, unimaginative
  Must learn to be more: enterprising, adaptable, forward-looking.

Adaptable, alert, experimental, inquisitive, gay, inconsistent, diffuse, *or*
unstable, impatient, restless, suggestible
  Must learn to: concentrate, relax, be more organised, be more sympathetic.

Month	Hour of birth	Ascendant sign
September	12 p.m. 1 a.m.	Cancer
September	2 a.m. 3 a.m.	Leo
September	4 a.m. 5 a.m. 6 a.m.	Virgo
September	7 a.m. 8 a.m. 9 a.m.	Libra

Nature

Cautious, emotional, parental, good mixer,
shrewd, tenacious, sensitive, *or*
self-pitying, exacting, niggling, touchy
   Must learn to: think clearly, control
emotions and imagination.

Ardent, magnanimous, pleasure-loving,
hospitable, flamboyant, theatrical, *or*
exuberant, demanding, indolent, predatory
   Must learn: humility, thrift, attention to
detail.

Practical, modest, sceptical, systematic,
impartial, conscientious, *or*
self-conscious, puritanical, unenthusiastic,
finicky
   Must learn to be: less narrow-minded,
more tolerant, more imaginative, more
optimistic.

Diplomatic, helpful, friendly, *or*
insincere, interfering, lazy, easily influenced,
dependent
   Must learn to be: firm, more decisive,
more consistent.

Month	*Hour of birth*	*Ascendant sign*
September	10 a.m. 11 a.m.	Scorpio
October	noon 1 p.m.	Capricorn
October	2 p.m. 3 p.m.	Aquarius
October	4 p.m.	Pisces

Nature

Incisive, intense, reserved, strong-willed, thorough, passionate, possessive, courageous, *or* ruthless, fanatical, jealous, secretive, suspicious, resentful, sensual

Must learn to: be more forgiving, control ambition and energy.

Fatherly, just, cautious, economical, dependable, self-absorbed, practical, *or* austere, severe, scrupulous, suspicious, mean, snobbish, morbid, uninspired

Must learn to: be more sociable, look on the bright side, cultivate better self-expression.

Intellectual, detached, scientific, humanitarian, unconventional, individualistic, *or* doctrinaire, remote, perverse, incalculable

Must learn to: have more warmth of feeling, cultivate the human touch, develop practical ability.

Easy-going, imaginative, suggestible, emotional, *or* lazy, unstable, chaotic, self-pitying

Must learn to: be more determined, concentrate, avoid alcohol and drugs.

Month	Hour of birth	Ascendant sign
October	5 p.m.	Aries
October	6 p.m. 7 p.m.	Taurus
October	8 p.m. 9 p.m.	Gemini
October	10 p.m. 11 p.m.	Cancer

Nature

Inspirational, impulsive, assertive, straightforward, sporting, *or* reckless, aggressive, naive

Must learn to: show moderation, be more tolerant, be more patient, show more forethought, show more humility.

Conservative, determined, patient, placid, deliberate, *or* reactionary, obstinate, stolid, lazy, unimaginative

Must learn to be more: enterprising, adaptable, forward-looking.

Adaptable, alert, experimental, inquisitive, gay, inconsistent, diffuse, *or* unstable, impatient, restless, suggestible

Must learn to: concentrate, relax, be more organised, be more sympathetic.

Cautious, emotional, parental, good mixer, shrewd, tenacious, sensitive, *or* self-pitying, exacting, niggling, touchy

Must learn to: think clearly, control emotions and imagination.

Month	Hour of birth	Ascendant sign
October	12 p.m. 1 a.m.	Leo
October	2 a.m. 3 a.m. 4 a.m.	Virgo
October	5 a.m. 6 a.m. 7 a.m.	Libra
October	8 a.m. 9 a.m.	Scorpio

Nature

Ardent, magnanimous, pleasure-loving,
hospitable, flamboyant, theatrical, *or*
exuberant, demanding, indolent, predatory
 Must learn: humility, thrift, attention to
detail.

Practical, modest, sceptical, systematic,
impartial, conscientious, *or*
self-conscious, puritanical, unenthusiastic,
finicky
 Must learn to be: less narrow-minded, more
tolerant, more imaginative, more optimistic.

Diplomatic, helpful, friendly, *or*
insincere, interfering, lazy, easily influenced,
dependent
 Must learn to be: firm, more decisive, more
consistent.

Incisive, intense, reserved, strong-willed,
thorough, passionate, possessive, courageous, *or*
ruthless, fanatical, jealous, secretive,
suspicious, resentful, sensual
 Must learn to: be more forgiving, control
ambition and energy.

Month	Hour of birth	Ascendant sign
October	10 a.m. 11 a.m.	Sagittarius

Nature

Honest, impulsive, jovial, speculative,
optimistic, alert, versatile, *or*
blunt, transparent, flighty, improvident,
over-confident, boisterous, dabbling, superficial

Must learn to be more: restrained, sincere,
thoughtful of others, purposeful.

3
THE TWELVE
ASCENDANT SIGNS

With Aries on the ascendant of your man's birth chart you can expect him to have the courage, initiative and optimism to carry you both through anything life throws at you. He does, however, need your wholehearted support, as he has a tendency to plunge into things and, if all does not go well, give up when success is just around the corner. He is never very good at thinking of the long-term result and readily discards good ideas in favour of something new and challenging that lacks the potential of a project he's already started.

Your Aries man needs success. He needs to be at the head of affairs, and in a position to issue orders and have them obeyed. Unfortunately, he may also adopt this attitude at home and with those nearest and dearest to him. You, his Girl-Friday, can follow one of two courses, and much depends on your own nature. If, for example, you happen to be Pisces, the problem will solve itself and you will almost certainly go along with his wishes and thank your stars that you have a man to take command of every situation. If, however, you are a Leo, then a husband, boyfriend, or boss who is too forceful – and Aries men can even be domineering – is going to upset your ego, and there could be trouble. Either way, you are not likely to win many arguments with this man. He relishes a direct confrontation. The symbol for Aries is the ram, a leader of the flock who will go on fighting any opposition to the end. Your Aries man won't give in.

As with the other fire signs, freedom to pursue his many interests is essential for your Aries man. Don't try to restrict his movements, don't fence him in; it won't work. He's a perpetual adolescent in that he can be very selfish and pays little regard to the feelings of others. But, while he can be difficult to live or work with and is as unpredictable as the wind, let anyone try to impose on you or make a pass at you and your Aries man will sort him out so quickly he will never know what hit him. This ram-type man is renowned for protecting his flock.

He invariably acts first and thinks afterwards, that is, if he ever stops to think at all. Just when you think he has settled down, you'll be up and away before you have time to finish your coffee, heading to where he thinks the pastures are greener and promotion a certainty. Unfortunately, his judgement can be faulty and his brilliant ideas and sudden whims can fall apart at the seams. One, two, or a dozen spectacular failures won't deter him, however. He never capitulates – defeat is a dirty word to an Aries man. One way or another he is going to be the boss. If initiative and enterprise are the ingredients for success, your man will have more than most.

When he was a kid he was probably up at the crack of dawn to deliver the milk, have a quick bite to eat and be off to deliver the morning papers. He wants money for the things it will buy him. You will rarely find an Aries man who is a saver, but neither does he waste what he earns. He knows that the only way to acquire something he wants is by hard work. There are no better workers than your Aries man, and he will expect you to put just as much into your partnership as he does.

Aries man has a fiery nature and is not always easy to live with. On the whole, women under the other fire signs, Leo and Sagittarius, and the air signs, Gemini, Libra, and Aquarius, are the most congenial partners for Aries.

Taurus man has his feet firmly fixed to the ground. He's a realist and the original son of the soil. Ever practical, an anchor of reliability, he possesses infinite patience.

Bearing in mind that a personal birth chart and horoscope is the only way to help you to really understand your man (this applies to all the zodiac types), I can say that a Taurus man generally makes the best husband.

He looks after his money, his possessions, his wife and his kids. He loves comfort and ease. Home comfort is his middle name and he would much rather wait until he can afford a thing of quality than buy something cheap. The cheap and shoddy offend his fine aesthetic sense of beauty and harmony.

He may not be the most exciting person in the world, and often appears stolid and uninteresting. An Aries man would sweep you off your feet to a future of excitement and constant uncertainty. Taurus, however, believes in sound finances, a secure home and a reliable partner; these are the cornerstones on which he seeks to build his future. He may not appeal to all women, but his love and devotion are unsurpassed. As ever, there is a price to pay. Your man has fanatical determination and is probably at the top of the league for pig-headed obstinacy. If you are the type for whom change and excitement are the breath of life, a Taurus man is not for you. You can beg and plead, but once he has made up his mind, nothing will change it – 'It's a matter of principle' is a Taurus man's favourite saying.

Law and order and the status quo are a kind of religion to him, and he is almost certain to be a dyed-in-the-wool conservative.

If your boss is a Taurus type, do not be misled into thinking he's a harmless old dear who wouldn't hurt a fly or say boo to a goose. Up to a point he is all these things – patience, remember, is his forte – and you can impose on his placid nature until you are lulled into thinking any old piece of sloppy work will do for him. But have a care, bulls have a nasty habit of trampling the object of their displeasure well and truly into the ground.

Deep down, your Taurus boyfriend is just the same. He will let you lead him wherever your fancy directs you, but, though he says little, he knows precisely what he's about and he's weighing you up every minute of the time. He can take ages in making up his mind and is in no hurry to dash down the aisle. He plays for keeps. 'For better, for worse, for richer, for poorer, until death you do part' could have been written by a Taurus man. When he makes his vows, your man means every single word of them.

He's a home bird, a fireside man, so don't expect him to spend his hard-earned money on exotica and far-away places, or you are going to be disappointed. His home really is his castle, and until it is paid for and as perfect as his innate good taste can make it, you won't be going far. He can comfortably make do with the greenhouse at the bottom of the garden. He loves peace and solitude and the satisfaction of growing things, and sees nothing wrong with you sitting knitting for the kids at your own fireside. He is the type of man thousands of women dream about.

Ideally, he is best suited with a partner under the signs of Cancer, Virgo and Capricorn.

Gemini

The sign of Gemini, the twins, symbolises two personalities in one, and quite often they are heading in different directions. Just when you think you understand this man, he does an about-turn and you are as confused as ever.

As far as you are concerned his greatest failing is his lack of warmth. His Taurus neighbour and, above all, Scorpio man are capable of consuming love and devotion. Your Gemini man, however, rarely experiences the extremes of human emotions, such as love and grief. He functions on a mental plane, influenced as he is by the planet Mercury, which we equate with communication in its various forms.

He is a great talker, a gossiper, always dashing here and there on lots of short journeys that are important to him. Variety and change are the spice of his life and the subjects which interest him are legion. He wants to know everything; where the butcher buys his meat, the life span of the Arctic Tern and how long a piece of string is. His curiosity is boundless, with the result that he never becomes an expert at anything. Your Gemini man is a great planner; unfortunately, his plans rarely progress beyond lists of what he requires. You may find that he has so many things he wants to do that he needs to keep lists of his lists.

A Gemini man tends towards nervous excitability because of his active mind. Your man has the best intentions, but they rarely come to anything. He is the most adaptable of men and has dabbled in many things. His nodding acquaintance with all kinds of jobs and subjects, and his ability to turn his hand to anything make it easy for him to change his job frequently.

His lack of warmth and feeling does have compensations inasmuch as you, his partner, will have a degree of freedom to do your own thing, which other zodiac types would not tolerate. He, of course, demands the same freedom for himself.

Many Gemini men are prone to flirting and you could

discover at some time that there is another woman in your man's life. But because of his lack of warmth he is unlikely to desert you; he just cannot get that deeply involved.

A Gemini man is not a good boss to work for. He is so unpredictable that you will never know quite where you stand with him. One day he is a martinet, the next he couldn't care less if you never did a stroke of work. Predicting his next move is the most futile pursuit. You will have to learn to live with his moods. He's just the type of man to drive a Virgo woman to distraction.

Your Gemini boyfriend could lead you a merry dance, too. He really means to pick you up at eight, but there are so many things that can attract his attention that more often than not he will be late, and occasionally he won't turn up at all. He needs a girlfriend for the companionship and conversation she can offer. The physical side of your relationship will be well down his list of priorities. If you are a warm and loving Pisces type, you have an uphill battle confronting you; your Gemini man tends to be all talk and no action.

Sharing your life with a Gemini man will never be uninteresting, but you may have to learn that you cannot go through life hanging on to his coat tails. He has got to be out and about doing something, anything. It can be very wearing and unless you are a Gemini, Leo or Sagittarian, you'd best leave him to get on with it. When he does come home he will have lots of interesting things to tell you and the cobbler's bill will be halved.

Cancer
Your Cancer man is highly sensitive. He needs the security of a good home and a partner to whom he can turn for

38

sympathy and understanding when he needs to withdraw from the stresses of earning a living. Outwardly he may appear to be as hard as nails, but he isn't really. Inside that hard shell he is soft and vulnerable.

He will fight and work for you and the kids until he drops from fatigue. You are the centre of his life, the very essence of the security he needs. His innate possessiveness makes him hang on to all that is his until his last breath. The symbol of Cancer is the crab; it never lets go once it takes hold.

He may be as good a husband as a Taurus man, but he is much more sensitive and subject to moods of depression if he thinks you are neglecting him. He may even be jealous of the affection you give the kids.

Like a Taurus man, he is very security-minded. As with everything else, he will tend to hang on to his money. He is the original 'rainy day' man and will quietly put away a bit each week. Unfortunately, he is not too keen to show it the light of day once it is in the bank. Knowing he has the cash should an emergency arise is another extension of his need for rock-like security.

Your Cancer man gives his loyalty unstintingly and you must do the same for him. He's a romantic, sentimental man. He loves to reminisce about the good times you have had in the past. The past is dear to him in other ways, too. His love and loyalty to his parents, and to yours, is very important; he will never let them down when they grow old or need help. He will almost certainly have an affinity for anything old and historical, and might collect relics that you would happily discard. The letters you wrote him when you were courting will be safely stowed away so that he can occasionally bring them out and relive those golden days.

His basic drive is to relate and be deeply involved with those with whom he comes in close contact. His family, friends and workmates are so much a part of his need to belong that should he lose any of them, it would be a blow that could make him retreat into his shell. In an extreme case he will wallow in self-pity.

Your Cancer boss, if you have one, will easily hide his sensitivity behind his hard outer shell. When it comes to making money, a Cancer man hasn't many equals and fewer superiors. For him, business is a very serious matter indeed, and he will expect you to follow his example. But it is worth remembering that a Cancer man is also sympathetic to those less fortunate than himself. Should misfortune befall you, you can count on his wholehearted support. You see, you too are one of his family. If you are loyal and hard-working, he will fight your battles and sort out your troubles as if you were his own son or daughter. He may never be the life and soul of the office party, but he will pick up the pieces when those less thoughtful have gone on to something that promises greater fun and excitement.

Your Cancer boyfriend is equally sensitive. His possessiveness may annoy you, but would you rather have a Gemini man who might turn up and then again might not? This boy is with you all the way, not wildly exciting perhaps, but utterly reliable. You can't have everything!

Generally, it can be said that Scorpio, Pisces and Capricorn women best suit a Cancer man.

Leo

Leo men are usually popular people. Your man just loves to be the centre of attention. His ready grin and friendly outgoing behaviour ensure that he has many friends. You may never cease to be amazed at the number of people he knows. The one thing he cannot stand is being ignored. Even as a child if he feels he is not getting the attention he merits, he will, in the last resort, make trouble to gain it.

Your Leo man may embarrass you, if you are a shy and retiring type, with such a commonplace thing as his mode of dress. Not for him the clerical grey and dark blue. He wants to be noticed, and what better to choose than a purple suit, a lime green shirt and an orange tie with socks to match! Remonstrate if you wish. Suggest something a little more sober and he could opt for green and purple checks, an orange shirt with lime green tie, and socks to match. If he is a flamboyant Leo, you cannot win.

He can be high-handed, domineering and bursting with boundless faith in himself. All these qualities may seem guaranteed to annoy you and everyone he meets, but it never seems to happen. There is something about your Leo man – his warm smile, his hail-fellow-well-met attitude – that, like the sun, his ruling planet, comes shining through to dispel all doubts about the genuine pleasure he exudes when he is with a crowd of people. He is intensely loyal to his friends and if you need someone to help fight your battles, your Leo man will always stand by you.

He has his faults, naturally. You will need to keep an account of your joint finances, as he spends very freely. His Cancer neighbour saves for a rainy day, but your Leo man spends money as if it was never going to rain again. A cautious Taurus woman may be prematurely grey trying to keep him in check.

Working for a Leo boss makes for an exciting life. He has the grand manner. His plans are ambitious and often impossible to achieve. Details bore him to tears and he will delegate you to plough through the paper work. The successes are his and the failures all yours. Just the same, you won't leave him. He's generous and if you want the day off, you need only ask; he finds it difficult to refuse anyone. It is also worth bearing in mind that a Leo man is easily flattered!

Your Leo boyfriend will take you dancing, to parties, dancing and to parties, until you don't know what day it is; a mad social whirl that will have you praying for a cosy evening by the fireside. He won't mind if you stay home as long as you don't want him to stay too. He lives life to the full; he works hard, plays hard and loves hard. A Leo man is often prone to heart troubles, and his women get circles under their eyes!

Your Leo husband, boyfriend, boss or kids do nothing by half measures; keeping pace with them rarely gives you time to worry or wonder. They always know where they are going, and that is to the top or centre of whatever they are involved in. It may be hard-going sometimes, but they have the strength and determination to take you along. Just hang on to this Leo man and you will not regret it. Your man is a bustling bundle of energy. He is usually best suited by an Aries or Sagittarius partner, and sometimes Gemini and Libra women can keep pace with him.

Virgo

Your Virgo man is something of a perfectionist. If you are the type who slops about until lunchtime in dressing gown and slippers trying to pluck up the courage or the energy to make a start with the housework, you are in trouble with this man for a partner. He is meticulous in habits, behaviour and appearance. To make matters worse, he has a finely-honed critical sense, which he is never shy of expressing.

Criticism of others less efficient than himself is probably the worst fault of every Virgo man. And, unfortunately, he is never loath to voice his disapproval. Your mother, the vicar, your neighbour, or anyone who does not measure up to his ideas of perfection could be on the receiving end of his displeasure.

A Pisces woman, for example, would loathe the kind of organisation a Virgo man needs to keep him happy. A place for everything and everything in its place.

Nonetheless, your Virgo man has many desirable qualities. You will never need to worry about unpaid bills or doors that have been off their hinges for months. He won't stay out half the night discussing philosophy, gamble his wages on the horses, or resort to drink or drugs when the going gets rough. You'll have no trouble with your kids either. They will do as they are told and if they want pocket money they will have to earn it doing chores about the house. A Virgo husband is not easily aroused to anger, he does not get frustrated with routine living, and he is deeply devoted to his partner in a calm, unemotional way. If you are ill, he will do the housework and look after you with down-to-earth efficiency – and do not be too offended if he does it rather better than you. As far as he is concerned, there are only two ways to do things, the right way and the wrong. It's true or it's false, it's black or it's white, but there are no shades of grey in your Virgo man's life.

You need to be good with money too. He will make a budget, so much for this and so much for that, and it has got to work. If it doesn't, he will want to know why, how, and where it went wrong. He has an analytical mind; facts, figures, and details are almost an obsession with Virgo men.

Your Virgo boss does not mince words. You do your job efficiently or you move on, of your own volition, more often than not. He does not suffer fools gladly. Don't, in a fit of tantrums, challenge him to do better; he may do just that. If, however, you have everything filed and know where to find it instantly, he can be a good man to have as a boss.

A Virgo boyfriend examines you microscopically. Your hairdo, your make-up, your hands, everything about you will be subjected to close investigation. Before you invite him back to your flat for coffee, mentally check that all was in order when you left. Ashtrays clean, the cap on the toothpaste replaced and no dishes left unwashed. If you are not too sure, put him off until you can find the time to have everything immaculate. He can be loving and attentive to your every wish, but he can demand a great deal in return. He wants a woman who is organised, efficient and beyond reproach. If he suggests how you can improve yourself in any way, you would do well to take note and not delay action to rectify your deficiencies. Aries, Leo and Sagittarius women are usually too impulsive for a Virgo man. He really needs a down-to-earth partner under the signs of Taurus or Capricorn. Women who are cautious and carefully organised best suit this meticulous man.

Libra

With Libra the ascendant sign in your man's birth chart, you may expect him to take the line of least resistance and adopt a philosophy of 'peace at any price'.

At face value this may seem a highly desirable trait in your partner's make-up, but there are times in everyone's life when decisions have to be made and action taken. Many women complain about having to make all the decisions and this is likely to be accentuated in the case of a Libra husband. Your man may be so concerned to do the right and fair thing that he becomes obsessed with weighing the pros and cons of a problem, and has great difficulty in making quite simple decisions. This dithering about could infuriate an Aries wife, even though she would quite enjoy having to take the initiative. A Pisces woman really needs a man capable of positive thought and forthright action, and a Libra partner would do nothing to shore up her moral.

Those under the sign of Libra are sometimes referred to as lazy Librans, but it is not necessarily true of them all. Much will depend on your man's sun sign and the influence of the other planets on his personality. An accurate assessment is only possible with an individual horoscope.

On the whole, Librans are easy-going people. Quite often you will find that they have an innate sense of beauty and harmony and a need to be at peace with the world. It is these Libran traits that have branded them as drifters who want to avoid conflict of any kind at any price.

There is, however, much to recommend this man as a partner. He loves home comforts and his aesthetic sense makes him an asset when his instinctive feeling for colour harmony is brought to bear on the problems of house decoration. You may find him asserting his authority, for once, when curtains, carpets and wall decorations have to be chosen.

Further to his credit is his concern about justice not only being done, but being seen to be done. The sign of Libra is the scales, symbolic of the judicial process. The weighing of facts, the sifting of evidence and a balanced judgement are very important to your Libra man. Although he detests conflict, if he sees injustice being done, he will step forward to restore the balance.

Unfortunately, his preoccupation with justice is such that he will rule against his own partner if that is what he feels is right. A Scorpio woman would find this very annoying, as she would expect undivided loyalty regardless of who was right and who was wrong.

Working for a Libra boss can be somewhat hazardous, as he has a reputation, not unwarranted, for being attractive to women. He is easy-going, a good talker, eager to please and very successful because of it. Asking you to work late could be the thin end of a well-calculated wedge! Back to business and true to type; getting him to make a clear-cut decision as to what he wants you to do may cause you frustration, especially if you are Aries.

A Libra boyfriend may sweep you off your feet with his natural charm and eagerness to please you, but there are few decisions that require more careful consideration than marriage, so be prepared for a long engagement. He may be indecisive, but if his easy-going personality appeals to you, he is well worth waiting for, especially if you are a Gemini or an Aquarius woman.

Scorpio

With Scorpio on the ascendant of your man's birth chart you are involved with perhaps the most powerful sign in the zodiac. Your Scorpio partner will always be a force to be reckoned with. He has unfathomable depths of passion. They may not have been released yet, but they are there – have no doubt about it. Like the scorpion, his zodiac symbol, he can wait with infinite patience; and when he strikes, the results can be devastating.

Your Scorpio man is capable of an intensity of feeling that no other sign in the zodiac can hope to emulate. He is, or can be, the type of lover most women only read of in novels.

Millions of women admire Richard Burton. When next

you see him in a film or on television, notice his eyes; eyes of mystery, daring you, beckoning you on. He is perhaps the best-known Scorpio man in the western world. Though your man may have little claim to fame, he, too, can fascinate lots of women. Fortunately, he is the most loyal zodiac type. If you can give him your love and affection unreservedly, you will have a man of whom you can be proud. He has tremendous will-power and is so secretive you might never know what he is thinking. If you betray him, his love will turn to hate. A Scorpio man can be so vindictive that he will destroy himself if that is the only way to have his revenge. There are no half measures with those under the influence of Scorpio.

His love and attention and all the finer feelings a man can have for a woman will send you spiralling onto a plane of experience you will never discover with other men. He is capable of bearing the pain and hardships of life to a degree that would have lesser men begging for mercy. He can take on jobs that are too tough, too unpleasant, or too dangerous for other people to tackle, and he will do them without a murmur of complaint. He is the type of man who carries his companions to safety against impossible odds. He would never desert you. He would rather die than admit defeat.

Your Scorpio boss is a force to be reckoned with. He wants your undivided devotion to him and the job he gave you. You may think him the greatest man you ever met, and so he is. But do not think that you will ever understand him. He, like all Scorpios, takes great care to hide his feelings and intentions. He will tell you what he thinks you ought to know and the rest will remain forever a mystery. He is as deep as the ocean and just as dangerous when roused. You can learn a lot from his calm, assured methods of tackling business problems. If you match his capacity for sheer hard

47

work, you have a boss second to none.

A Scorpio boyfriend may be something of a problem in-asmuch as he will try to dominate you. If you are the type – an Aquarian, for example – who does not take kindly to being led, you will soon be minus a boyfriend. He must be the leader and you the follower. Like his married brother, he will do anything to win you, more by actions than words. You will be in no doubt that you are the one for him when he makes up his mind. You do not 'catch' a Scorpio man. He is too shrewd to fall for female flattery and will, in any case, resent it. Your Scorpio man is nobody's fool, and has enough inborn romantic finesse to recognise your intentions almost as soon as you formulate them in your mind. If you are the right girl, he will decide for himself, as he decides everything in his life where a degree of personal control is possible, quite coolly and often calculatingly. Cancer, Pisces and, to a lesser degree, Taurus, Virgo and Capricorn women should find a Scorpio man very good for them.

Sagittarius

You will rarely be bored by anyone with a strong Sagittarian influence in his birth chart. With a Sagittarius ascendant dominating his personality, you have a man with enough optimism to carry you both through any adversities that may come your way. Life with him will always be interesting if you can bear with his sudden whims. You may just be settling down to sleep when he nudges you and says, 'It's a lovely night, let's go to the beach.' The fact that it's midnight and the beach is fifteen miles away is of no consequence to your man. He will do the craziest things when you least expect them. Should you be a sober-sided and serious Capricorn woman, you may not find his bubbling enthusiasm for everything he does much to your liking. This man of yours is a born gambler who will take a chance on anything. He could well toss up a promising career to do something he feels is more worth while; that he is cutting his salary by half won't trouble him at all. Money means little to your Sagittarian man. Whether he has a lot or little of it, he will find innumerable ways to be rid of it, not all of them sensible.

He really needs someone to look after him. A money-conscious partner who can manage his affairs without restricting his sense of freedom, adventure, and constant quest for knowledge would be good for him. You may always need to hold him in check and it will never be easy. His enthusiasms, which can be many and varied, with most of them short-lived, can try the patience of a saint.

He needs to be out and about, and his views of what is permissible for a married man will be intolerable to many women. It does not improve matters when you discover that he does not always want you with him. However, you have in your Sagittarian a man who will not seek to restrict your freedom if you feel you would like to go out and carve a career for yourself. He will probably admire you for it.

Your Sagittarian partner is intensely loyal, but he will insist that he is free to follow his many interests without restriction. This means so much to him that in the last resort he would leave you rather than have someone who cannot match his broadminded outlook on life.

Life with a Sagittarian boss can be trying – he's so unpredictable that you may never be sure from one day to the next what he will do. You may even think of him as a likeable nutcase. One thing you will soon discover is that if he thinks it, he says it. 'You have gorgeous legs' may be followed immediately by 'You did say you went to typing

49

school?' as he surveys you and your work with mixed feelings. He is rarely where he ought to be. You will like him so much that you find yourself making excuses for him as he rushes around doing next week's work while last week's lies on his desk neglected or forgotten. His enthusiasms wax and wane with an unnerving disregard for priorities. He is an exciting man to work for if you don't mind variety and change mixed with uncertainty and bewilderment.

A Sagittarian boyfriend can be interesting, exciting, loving and loyal, but tying him down might be a long and tedious process. He will be in no hurry to get married. There are many things he wants to do before settling down and the list will be just as long, if somewhat different, fifty years later. If you are the type of girl who envisages living just around the corner from Mum, you may have chosen the wrong boy. A Sagittarian loves to travel and, whether it be Borneo or Beckenham, you must be prepared to go wherever his interests lead him – and do not rule out the moon. His ambitions are always set high. If you can back him all the way, he'll reach for the stars. Aries and Leo women are the most congenial partners for a Sagittarian.

Capricorn

If Capricorn is on the ascendant of your man's birth chart, life with him is unlikely to be one wild round of pleasure. He is too concerned with making a living, climbing the ladder of success, and maintaining high standards by hard work and good behaviour.

In many ways your Capricorn man is like Taurus, but he is more motivated by ambition and more serious-minded. His brand of ambition is of a cautious, plodding type; there is nothing meteoric about this man. There are undoubtedly more exciting men to be had than a Capricorn, but on the whole you can equate excitement with uncertainty, and caution with peace of mind. So much depends on what you want out of life.

This man is no great lover. 'Darling' and 'sweetheart' are endearments you will have to learn to live without. To him life is far too serious a business to go rushing around wearing his heart on his sleeve. Valentine cards would soon go out of fashion if Capricorn men were the only customers. Hard work is his middle name. He goes to bed with caution and has discipline for breakfast, and he might expect you to adopt the same mode of living. A Leo wife would find him very inhibiting, as she so loves to enjoy herself among a crowd of people with similar tastes.

Your Capricorn man usually makes a slow start in life. It takes him ages to get steam up, but all the time he is coolly calculating in which direction he ought to travel. That it will be up the ladder of success is a very safe bet, and his ladder will be sunk well into the ground and tied securely at the top. He does not advance until he is sure he can retreat in complete safety should he discover he has made a mistake, which, I hasten to add, is unlikely. Your Capricorn man is a very astute person; he invariably knows precisely where he is going and why.

Hard work, they say, never killed anyone, which may have something to do with Capricorn people being noted for their longevity.

Your Capricorn boss is a dedicated man. He will be at the office before you arrive and will lock up at night long after everyone has gone home. Working with him is a pleasure if you like your work. He's quiet and efficient. You won't get much praise for your efforts and he won't expect any from you. In time you will come to appreciate this man as a boss who knows what he wants and how to get it without fuss or histrionics. There is nothing about your boss to make you swoon with love and admiration, but slowly and surely he will gain your respect as a man who does his job supremely well. Your loyalty, which is all he wants from you, you will give wholeheartedly; he is that kind of a man.

A Capricorn boyfriend may be hovering on the outer edge of your circle of friends for ages before you notice him. He has made up his mind that you are the girl for him, but he doesn't know quite how to make an approach and ask you for a date. If you like him, it will save a great deal of time if, just this once, you do the asking. There will be no rave-ups with this boy; it is not in him to want to hit the highspots. If you want quiet devotion, holding hands for hours with little conversation, and complete confidence, you have a boyfriend second to none. Taurus and Virgo girls best suit this quiet, ambitious man.

Aquarius

The Aquarian ascendant in your man's birth chart, you may discover, exerts an increasing degree of influence on his character as he gets older.

Aquarians are perhaps the most difficult people to understand. If your man seems to live in a world of his own and show little concern for the everyday problems of living, it is typical Aquarian behaviour. He tends to think in the broadest possible terms and is concerned with the conditions of humanity as a whole. Making a success of life at a mundane level holds little attraction for this man.

The ordinary drives and ambitions that most of us have are quite often completely lacking in an Aquarian man.

Your man, more than any other, requires freedom, freedom of thought and freedom of action. In an extreme case, especially if you bring too much pressure to bear on him and demand that he makes a real effort to acquire a fine house and two cars, he could be driven to opt out of society. He can take the view that the rat race and all it entails are goals of very doubtful value.

Push this man of yours against his better judgement and one day he may walk out on you without so much as a backward glance or a moment's regret. Trying to argue or reason with him is rather like fighting a shadow – a complete waste of time.

He can be a great disappointment to women under the more ambitious signs, such as Aries, Leo, Virgo and Capricorn. They, more than others, will have great difficulty understanding and making allowances for his lack of interest in acquiring the trappings of wealth; he genuinely doesn't need them. An Aquarian husband is one of the most misunderstood men in the world. He will have no objection to your going out and carving a career for yourself as long as you don't expect him to get involved. It is, however, in his favour that should you need to get out and about meeting people with the same ideas and values as your own, your Aquarian man is unlikely to raise any objections.

You may never experience the deep emotional involvement with this man that you would with a Taurus or Scorpio. What he really needs is a partner who shares his ideals and values, a woman who can express herself lucidly and is not too concerned with the physical relationship that means so much to many women.

If you work for an Aquarian boss, you may have to nurse him along. He can be absent-minded and completely unpredictable. If you have been with him more than six months, you may be close to creating a record. 'How did he ever get the job?' is a question you will often ask yourself.

But what you need to remember is that an Aquarian boss is a very rare bird indeed, and may himself wonder how he ever got into such a mess. The rat race is not for an Aquarian, and, if you stay long enough, you will see him leave when he realises that it was all a terrible mistake.

An Aquarian boyfriend may be a great disappointment to you. He won't be in a hurry to name the day. Concealing your true intentions will call for skill and diplomacy, as he would rather not get emotionally involved with anyone. He may think you will make demands on him that he cannot fulfil, and this includes the physical side of your relationship. He doesn't really want anything but companionship. Long chats on religion and philosophy will always be preferable to torrid necking sessions. Taurus, Scorpio and Pisces women could be very frustrated with this man for a boyfriend.

Pisces

With a Pisces ascendant dominating your man's birth chart you may have a dreamer for a partner. He could live in an emotional world of make-believe. Not only will he love you, but he might worship the ground you walk on. It may sound marvellous to many women, but the price of his adoration could be higher than you anticipate. A Pisces man can be notoriously weak in character. He can stagger from one situation to another without the vaguest notion of how to get out of them. If your womanly instinct demands that you have a partner who leads and protects you, then you could be very disappointed with this man for a mate.

Your Pisces man has boundless compassion. If you are worried or hurt, you won't have to tell him; he is a human receiving station, ultra-sensitive to your desires and wishes. Suffering of any kind is his personal burden. The danger is that he is also aware of other people's feelings and can become so involved with helping them that he may neglect you. He seldom gets his priorities right. He can lose sleep trying to make the tiniest decision, which can be very annoying for a partner with a forceful, decisive personality.

He is marvellous where children are involved. He finds it easy to come down to their level, and their make-believe world is his, too. When flying a kite together, they have the Concorde on the other end of the string, and an old piece of wood floating on a pond is magically transformed in their imaginations to the Q.E.2.

It is a wonderful world, but your Pisces man needs to earn a living. If fate decrees him to be a factory worker, his innate creativity can be crushed and he may not have the determination to change things for the better. Money matters and the routine of day-to-day living can be almost beyond his comprehension. He may drift on this sea of reality like a ship without a rudder.

What your man needs is a perfect world where everyone is kind and understanding, where wars and famine could never happen, and cruelty is unknown. You may always have to take the initiative with a Pisces man for a partner.

A Pisces boss, like an Aquarian, is a rare bird. The cut and thrust of commerce is usually too much for him, and if he does make the grade, it is probably due to some very dominant factor in his birth chart. For example, if you discover that your boss has a Pisces ascendant, you should carefully reconsider his sun sign. It is the latter that will have driven him to gain a position of authority. Alternatively he could have a powerful Mars in authoritative Leo, close to the mid-heaven. This will often account for traits that are not immediately apparent without the knowledge gained from the study of a personal horoscope.

A Pisces boyfriend can be a pathetic figure when he falls

in love. He moons about dreaming of you and wishing you could be with him constantly. You will have no trouble in persuading him to marry, but, in view of what I have said, you should be very sure that he is the right man for you. Marry in haste and repent at leisure is something you should have firmly fixed in your mind when your boyfriend has a Pisces ascendant. This is especially true if you are a down-to-earth Taurus, Virgo or Capricorn. He needs a down-to-earth partner to guide and advise him, but you could become very upset if you have to take the lead in everything you do together.

4
LIBRA
WITH
ASCENDANT SIGNS

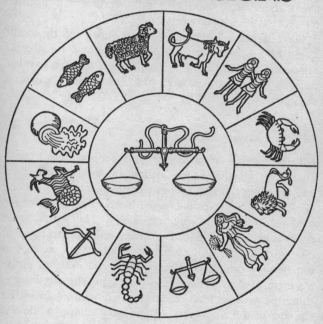

Libra with Aries ascendant

This is a fortunate combination of the sun in Libra and ascendant Aries. The self-assertiveness and driving initiative of Aries is balanced by the charm and easy-going ways of Libra. Compromise is at the base of the Libran desire to be all things to all men. By itself it can spell weakness of character, a peace-at-any-price approach to living. Libra needs the Aries qualities of self-assertion and positive thought to stiffen his character.

Combine these Libra and Aries qualities and the result might be a person with a positive drive and a degree of self-assurance. Add the Libra willingness to listen to other people's points of view and you could have a balanced character.

Libra with Taurus ascendant

Unless there is some strong disruptive aspect in this man's birth chart, he will be a man with whom most women could live very happily. His Libran need for complete harmony in all his relationships is boosted by the Taurus desire for total security for his wife and family. This man's home really is his castle. He loves comfort, and his natural good taste ensures that he will make you a home of which you can be very proud. He is easy-going and eager to please his mate. If she is a freedom-loving type, she can do anything she wishes within reason. He will willingly look after the kids and help with the household chores while she carves out a career or pursues her particular interests. If this is your man, you can consider yourself very fortunate.

Libra with Gemini ascendant

This man is unlikely to make an ideal husband. He certainly falls very far short of the Libra–Taurus man, for example. The Libra influence indicates a man who finds it difficult to make decisions, and the Gemini influence could prevent his sustained concentration. A mixture of these traits makes him a keen conversationalist who loves to be out and about; he could be a comparative stranger to his partner. A pure Libra man is usually very loving, but Gemini finds it difficult to feel deeply about anyone. The result could be a person who constantly confuses his partner as his moods blow hot and cold. This man needs a woman with saintly patience who enjoys being on her own most of the time.

Libra with Cancer ascendant

A combination of Libra and Cancer traits makes this man a very desireable partner for the majority of women. He is easy-going, good company, eager to please his partner and very concerned that she should be happy and feel secure. If he has a fault, it may manifest itself through Cancer's possessiveness; he could be a little reluctant to grant his mate the degree of freedom some women need. One of Libra's most important traits, however, is his understanding of other people's views and desires. He will always accede to reasonable requests, so that possessiveness may not be a factor to cause friction. An Aries woman could spoil her partnership with this man through her aggressiveness.

Libra with Leo ascendant

There are not many women who could not get along with this fun-loving, easy-going man. The Leo influence on his character makes him friendly and out-going, a man who enjoys life because he gives much more than he takes. The Libra trait of desiring peace and harmony makes him the kind of person who is everybody's friend. He brings the warmth of the sun into people's lives. No one is perfect, however, and if this Libra–Leo man has a fault, it could be that his attitude to life is rather too relaxed for serious-minded women with ambition. Virgo and Capricorn women could feel frustrated by his lack of application and ambition.

Libra with Virgo ascendant

In this quite good combination of sun and ascendant sign, the Libra influence will do much to soften the Virgo ascendant qualities. Most women should have little difficulty in making a success of a partnership with this man. He may never achieve any great success because Libra is too easy-going and Virgo prefers to stay in the background. He could be the typical 'man in the street', who loves his wife and kids, has a steady job, and is content with his home comforts. He probably won't be an exciting partner – he won't want to rush you off to the ends of the earth in search of adventure. But he also won't have you wondering how you are going to pay the electricity bill or where the money for the children's shoes is to come from, and there are plenty of men like that. If you are looking for a partner, you could do much worse than choose a Libra–Virgo man.

Libra with Libra ascendant

This double Libra man will be charming, but so easy-going that many women could be frustrated by his disinclination to exert himself. He might be a man who makes many promises that he never fulfils. He hates conflict and will always agree with you when you complain about his laxity. He will vow that tomorrow he will turn over a new leaf, and be more convinced than you that it shall be so. It is almost impossible to argue with him when he agrees with you, but life with him could be one long battle to make him live up to his responsibilities. Women who need a great deal of personal freedom may be the only ones who could make some sort of success of a partnership with this man. Gemini and Aquarius women, for example, might make a go of it.

Libra with Scorpio ascendant

A Libra–Scorpio man has many qualities that appeal to the majority of women, but his attraction may not be so desirable when he is one woman's man. Libra and Scorpio combined could produce a man who will rarely hesitate to take advantage of all the women who fall in love with him. Through Libra's influence he is easy-going, charming, and often good looking. Add the Scorpio air of mystery and powerful sex drive and you could have a partner who needs constant surveillance. More positively, Scorpio drive and determination should give a useful boost to Libra's lack of ambition. He is a man who could go far, but there is always a danger that he might go without you when the opposition is young and alluring.

Libra with Sagittarius ascendant

If you want a partner who is very willing to let you do as you please, this could be the man for you. Libra's influence can make him charming, good-looking and lazy. Sagittarius adds a strong gambling instinct, a sense of adventure and an irrepressible optimism that makes him confident that the arrival of the bailiffs tomorrow will be postponed by a set of fortuitous circumstances. For example, we might be invaded by men from Mars. The Libra–Sagittarius man needs a wife who is intent on pursuing a career, and, preferably a career that pays well. This happy-go-lucky man would have Taurus, Cancer, Virgo, Scorpio, Capricorn and possibly Pisces women prematurely grey-haired. An Aries partner would fight with him, but Gemini and Aquarius women could probably get along with him, as they are invariably too engrossed in their own interests to let a man worry them too much.

Libra with Capricorn ascendant

If the Libra and Capricorn characteristics are well-balanced, this man should be a reliable, predictable and good partner for most women. He might not be a very exciting partner, but Libra's easy-going approach to life will be considerably stiffened by Capricorn's quiet determination to ensure security through hard work and cautious ambition. This man is probably a home bird, and Libra's flair for creating a comfortable and pleasant environment should be an incentive for his partner to stay at home too. A man with Capricorn strong in his birth chart is inclined to believe that a woman's place is in the home. This man will not encourage you to go out to work or to have other outside interests.

Libra with Aquarius ascendant

This is a combination of two air signs, which denotes a man who is mentally active and communicative. He could be almost entirely motivated to promoting harmony, truth and knowledge as values for the affluent society to adopt. He needs a partner who is essentially a companion with similar interests, a woman who prefers a mental rather than a physical relationship. This Libra–Aquarius man may be a great disappointment to many women, as he could lack ambition and a fine home with two cars may not figure at all in his list of priorities. Gemini, Sagittarius and Aquarius women would probably regard him as a partner worth having.

Libra with Pisces ascendant

A combination of two relatively weak signs could endow this man with more than his fair share of human weaknesses. He could, however, have an exceptionally well-developed aesthetic sense, which might lead to success in some art form. If you are the type of woman who needs a man to take the initiative in all that you do together, this Libra–Pisces man could be a great disappointment. He needs a partner to encourage and direct him to make the most of his talent. A Scorpio or Capricorn woman might suit him best.

5
LIBRA
MAN AND WOMEN
THROUGH THE ZODIAC

When reading the following interpretations of Libra man as a mate for women under the twelve zodiac signs, it is important to realise that the outline of traits of each couple can only give a general indication of compatibility. A personal horoscope is necessary to determine the proper marriage partner for a particular person. Marriage is a partnership, and if it is to survive and flourish there must be give and take on both sides. Astrology can highlight the areas of possible friction. Knowing what the problems are likely to be, both partners can ensure, by working together and understanding each other, that they will never allow themselves to reach a point where they can disrupt their marriage.

Libra man and Aries woman

This can be a good partnership, but much may depend on the amount of effort your Libra partner puts into it.

On the whole he is easy-going, and hates discord of any kind, so you will need to curb your fiery Aries temper.

A possible area of disharmony in your partnership could arise from your man not being very ambitious. You are full of ambitious plans, and your energy and drive will almost certainly far exceed your partner's. When opportunities to advance your social and financial prestige present themselves, you will want to rush ahead, confident that here at last is the chance you have been awaiting for so long.

Unfortunately, your Libra man is not inclined to rush anywhere; he is too easy-going and too anxious to weigh the pros and cons of the situation. Persuading him to make a decision could annoy you very much. But, in fact, this trait of his could be to your advantage, as Aries people are very impatient and seldom stop to think. Like the other fire signs, Leo and Sagittarius, you act first and think later. You are very good at making snap decisions, but many of them are bad ones.

Together you both have qualities that, sensibly combined, could make a happy and successful partnership. There is nothing wrong in gently nudging your Libra man along the lines you want him to follow, but you will only make him unhappy if you become too impatient. He is so genuinely concerned to please you that too much pressure would make him concede to your demands against his better judgement. More often than not he will prove to be right and then you may wish you had listened.

Your love life should present no problems, as Libra love and Aries ardency should ensure a satisfying relationship.

Libra man and Taurus woman

A Libra man–Taurus woman partnership has every chance of being successful because both of you are easy-going people.

If there is any area of disagreement in your relationship it may spring from your differing attitudes to work.

With Taurus dominant in your birth chart, security is very high on your list of priorities. Economic security is usually only achieved by hard work, which Taurus people never shirk. Your Libra man, however, may be less inclined to make the effort. Although you are a very patient woman, if your man persists in not pulling his weight, trouble could ensue. That, I hasten to add, is most unlikely to happen. A Libra partner is invariably motivated towards peace and harmony, and if this man of yours feels that making more effort will result in your happiness and well-being, he will rise to the occasion.

In all other respects, you have much the same aims and desires. Your home, for example, is tenanted by two people with intuitive good taste in furniture and all the decorative arts. Regardless of your income, your home will be an example of how comfortable and pleasant surroundings can be contrived without spending a fortune.

Your joint finances must inevitably be left in your capable Taurus hands. Your mate, while not being as wasteful as some, is not one to deny himself pleasures that he cannot really afford.

Your love life should be very happy, as your earthy appreciation of physical pleasures will be much appreciated by your Libra partner.

It is difficult to envisage this partnership being anything but a great success.

Libra man and Gemini woman

This partnership could encounter some difficulties, and adjustments to allow for your differing characteristics will be required before you achieve success.

Disharmony is most likely to arise from a lack of consistency in both parties. If things do go wrong, it is more than likely that you are equally to blame.

Both Libra and Gemini are air signs and traditionally you have much in common. For example, you are both adaptable, friendly souls, who enjoy talking to and meeting people; you are both sociable and easy to get along with. But a successful partnership needs much more than this. You have a home to run, bills to pay and money to earn. Perhaps most important of all, someone has to lead this duo and each of you would prefer to leave it to the other.

A Gemini woman is not usually interested in diligent

domesticity. You tend to regard the day-to-day chores as tiresome routine that prevents you getting out and about in pursuit of your many interests. Your Libra mate thrives on pleasant surroundings, and wants a well-run, comfortable home. He would prefer, however, that someone else did the work. Obviously this is a situation that must be solved to your mutual satisfaction. Your partnership demands that you both assume a fair share of your joint responsibilities and carry them out conscientiously. If you can do this, you are well on the way to achieving the success that astrological tradition assigns to a Libra-Gemini partnership.

Your Libra man is loving and always concerned to make you happy; indeed, he would be miserable if you were discontent. A Gemini woman is often lacking in deep affection, and your love life may require some adjustments before it can be mutually satisfying.

Even so, there is nothing to prevent a successful partnership if you both make the effort to really share your responsibilities.

Libra man and Cancer woman

There should be no great problems to solve before a Libra–Cancer partnership is quite successful.

There may be no such thing as a perfect marriage, but you two should get along very well together once you appreciate your differing characteristics and make the effort to adjust to them.

In most partnerships defining areas of a relationship that could give rise to disharmony is usually fairly simple, but in your case there is nothing really tangible – it is something sensed rather than something known.

It may be that basically you are both people who need

someone to lead and direct you. Your Libra man may lack firmness and be indecisive while you are swayed by your emotions and can be quite illogical when deeply involved. These traits in themselves could add up to a very loving couple, with each partner concerned to ensure the happiness of the other. But underlying your devotion there may be a lack of leadership that could make you drift aimlessly on a sea of mutual admiration.

This partnership's success may depend on Cancer's need for security assuming the power to direct your joint efforts towards economic stability. You probably have an innate shrewdness in such affairs, which could be vital to your success. Your Libra man is easy-going, but he never refuses to listen to, and carefully weigh, advice given him. When he realises that you are working for your mutual good, he will do as you advise.

Your financial affairs should never be a cause for concern as long as Cancer holds the reins.

Cancer people are very loving, but you can be too possessive. Your Libra man needs a degree of freedom, as do the other air signs, Gemini and Aquarius. Your love life should always be a very important and satisfying part of your relationship, one which will sustain you through the trials and tribulations of life.

Libra man and Leo woman

This couple should have no great difficulty in making a success of their partnership.

Your Libra man can get along with almost anyone because of his innate friendliness. He hates fighting and arguing. A Libran has a good natured attitude towards life, which he is aware is too short to spoil with constant bickering.

Leo people have many things in common with Librans. You enjoy life to the full – if other people will let you – and are never happier than when you are able to make others happy. A busy social life gives you the opportunity to shine like the sun, your ruling planet. Your Libra partner is equally happy as a homebird or a socialite; his main concern is to please you.

There is, however, one area of contention between you that could spoil your relationship if you allow it: the sensible management of your domestic affairs, especially where money is concerned. As you probably know, this is one of the most common causes of friction in marriages.

Your Libra partner is never loath to spend money on pleasure and comfort. And you, let's face it, are not much better; probably worse if anything. It would be best to have your bills paid through your bank or by some other agent with a greater respect for money than either of you possess.

Leo people are often very ambitious and have the drive and ability to work hard for what they want. Your Libra partner is much more content to take what life brings along, providing it is not too arduous or uncomfortable. If you do aspire to greater things, you may have to push your man along, and there is nothing wrong in that, within reason. What you should guard against is slipping into the role of a domineering female, which some Leo women do, especially if they have a mate who is basically weak.

Your love life should be a very satisfying part of your relationship, as Leo's warmth and Libra's eagerness to please is a combination that must be successful.

This partnership must go well if you organise your domestic affairs with efficiency and Leo does not dominate.

There may be some problems to solve before this couple can make a success of their relationship.

The most probable area of contention for you two may arise out of your differing attitudes towards your domestic affairs.

Virgo's whole life seems dedicated to hard work and efficiency, and you have an unerring eye for those who do not measure up to your exacting standards. Add to this your readiness to criticise and life at home for your peace-at-any-price Libra mate could be very far from what he desires.

To your easy-going Libra man, life is a pleasure and home is somewhere to relax in comfort. He loves to have friends in for a meal followed by interesting discussions that allow him the opportunity to practise looking at all sides of a problem and producing a balanced judgement.

'And what good will that do?' is a typical down-to-earth Virgo rejoinder. You do not have the time to indulge in speculation, especially when you cannot see how it will achieve anything. But life at home will be much more pleasant if just occasionally you learn to relax and enjoy yourself. Your Libra man will be happier too. All work and no play can make Jill a very dull girl and difficult to live with! Your man will do anything for you, within reason. Don't spoil him with nagging.

In spite of these problems, there is a good deal in favour of your partnership. Basically your are both home-lovers. Neither of you is particularly ambitious, so the conflict that frequently arises when partners have widely differing degrees of ambition should not trouble you. Financial affairs will never be a problem when Virgo is in charge, and your Libra man is loath to raise objections about anything.

Your love life should be quite satisfying, as your Libra man can adjust to any partner.

The degree of success this partnership enjoys could be in direct proportion to Virgo's willingness to concede that there is more to life than hard work.

Libra man and Libra woman

This should be a good partnership, as you, naturally, have much in common. However, wherever a double sign is involved you should pay special attention to your individual ascendant sign qualities, which should help you both to understand any traits that are not typical of Libra.

By many people's standards you can be regarded as a couple who failed to make the grade. But their standards are not yours, as Librans have a desire to enjoy life and think it is best done by not becoming involved in the rat race to financial and social success. In the long run your kind of success, which is called happiness, is something that more materially-motivated people may never possess.

The greatest threat to the kind of life you both want is a mishandling of your financial affairs.

Libra people love luxury. You have a flair for all forms of home decoration and this extends to your personal wardrobes. It all adds up to expensive tastes, but neither of you has much desire to work to pay for them. You are the kind of couple who could become enmeshed in the hire purchase net. You will never have any trouble convincing each other that you really do need that new suite to make your sitting room perfect.

Your Libra man is quite happy to share the housework and will do it well, as untidiness makes him uncomfortable. You, in turn, could do something to bolster your tottering

72

finances by getting a job. You would enjoy advising customers on what clothes suited them best. Of course, your boss might not be quite so happy, as your concern for what suited the customer would not always be conducive to sales.

Your love life should be a very successful part of your relationship, as Libra people are very concerned to please their partners.

With a modicum of common sense about what you can and cannot afford, your partnership could be a great success.

Libra man and Scorpio woman

This is a partnership between an easy-going man and a very strong-willed woman. Fortunately, you both have qualities that could be combined to make a successful and happy couple.

A Scorpio woman's dedication to her mate's well-being is unsurpassed and if the same could be said of your Libra man then you would have no problems at all.

You are an ambitious woman with a massive determination to achieve your goals. You will help your Libra partner build an empire, or, if he falls foul of your displeasure, you will crush him.

The main danger to your relationship is that Libra men are often handsome, dress well, have charming manners and are attractive to most women.

If your man is typically Libra, he quite enjoys the attention women lavish on him. Nothing is more guaranteed to infuriate Scorpio, and your jealousy can be very destructive. You should remember that your Libra man is unlikely to want to go off with any other woman; the plotting and scheming required is too much trouble for this man. Peace and goodwill is something your Libra man works for, and he will rarely jeopardise this hard-won harmony.

Your domestic affairs should never be a bone of contention, as a Scorpio woman is a very capable housewife and financier. Your Libra partner's penchant for over-spending has no chance of getting out of control with you in charge.

Your love life will be the kind that many couples can only read about in books. They might even want to consult a couple of experts like you for advice.

If your Libra man can contribute the kind of effort that a Scorpio woman expects of her partner, you will see to it that your partnership is a complete success.

Libra man and Sagittarius woman

This partnership of a Libra man and a Sagittarius woman should be quite successful, if somewhat precarious.

A Sagittarian's idea of keeping house may not measure up to your Libra partner's requirements. He loves a home that is uncluttered and comfortable, but you have little inclination to get bogged down by the boring, necessary chores that make this possible.

You are both easy-going people, but money mismanagement could cause trouble between you. Your Libra man can dispose of his money with consummate ease in pursuit of luxury and comfort. With you for a partner, your financial affairs could soon run into serious trouble. Sagittarians are born optimists and really believe that something will turn up to save the day. As a couple, you should leave your financial obligations in the hands of someone who can ensure that you do not overspend.

Being a Sagittarian, you are a freedom-lover and need to have time to go out, probably to meetings that have an intellectual bias. So often fire sign women have varying degrees of trouble to win some time to themselves so that they can meet new people, learn new things, and get away from the daily grind that threatens to dull their active minds. With a Libra man for a partner, you can count yourself very lucky. Not only is he easy-going, but, even more important, he can appreciate your point of view and will willingly look after the kids while you go to your night class. In return, you could make just a bit more effort to ensure his comfort at home.

Your love life should always be a very satisfying part of your relationship. Libra 'air' and Sagittarius 'fire' ensure real warmth!

You could be one of those couples who find a niche that is neither too demanding nor too stultifying. Take more care over money and you should be very happy.

Libra man and Capricorn woman

This partnership may have some adjustments to make before it can be counted a success.

A Capricorn woman can be austere, ambitious, and practical, an attitude to life that is very different to your Libra partner's.

He is easy-going, pleasure-loving and rarely ambitious. He much prefers to drift through life, which is centred on a comfortable home, lots of interesting friends and not too much work.

At first sight there may seem to be irreconcileable traits, but things are seldom as bad as they appear to be.

You are a very patient woman, one who can spend much of her life gradually moulding and manipulating circumstances so that in the end you achieve whatever you set out to do.

Your Libra man is very susceptible to manipulation; he is eager to please and hates disharmony. His indecisiveness could benefit from your quiet determination. You can do much to guide this man of yours, but you must not let Capricorn's cold, calculating ways spoil what can be a very warming relationship. Give him your respect and he will quite happily comply with your wishes. He will soon learn to appreciate that you can help him acquire the comfort he needs, and his fair-mindedness will concede that somebody has to push if he is ever going to achieve some success.

Your domestic and financial affairs will never be a bone of contention. Your Libra man would readily rid himself of the money he earns – and he is not very good at spending it wisely – but the problem will never arise with a capable Capricorn woman in charge.

Your love life should not present any serious incompatibility, as your Libra man will be quite happy to adjust to your desires.

This partnership's success depends very much on Capricorn's common sense.

Libra man and Aquarius woman

This could be a quite successful partnership. Your compatibility will always be on the mental rather than physical plane.

In your different ways you are both easy-going people and, as long as you allow each other a fair degree of freedom, you should get along together very well.

There are, however, two possible areas of conflict that require early solutions.

Your Libra man is more concerned with his own ease and comfort than with those who are less fortunate than himself. He has little inclination to alleviate the misfortunes of others, but this is something often high on the Aquarian's list of priorities. There may always be a danger that you will despise your Libra man for what you regard as selfishness. A Libran in rarely selfish. He is just very easy-going, and you cannot change this. Be thankful that you have a partner who understands your concern, even though he does not feel it himself.

Your domestic organisation is the other bone of contention. But again your Libra man is willing to help. The daily round of domestic chores quickly disenchants an Aquarian woman. You try to understand what life is about, and soon conclude that it is not about dusting, decorating and drudgery. If you make some effort to ensure the comfort that your man loves, he will be very willing to lend a hand in the home and so give you the opportunity to follow your interests.

Many marriages slowly grind to a halt when the partners no longer have much to say to each other, but yours is not likely to be one of them. Your Libra man loves to talk, to argue the pros and cons of any subject in search of a balanced judgement. He may not agree with you, but he is prepared to listen and to try to understand your point of view.

Your love life should be quite satisfactory as neither of you is likely to make demands the other cannot fulfil.

Your relationship may never be successful in material terms, but it has many worthwhile qualities that others are sadly lacking.

Libra man and Pisces woman

Both of you so readily make allowances for the weakness of

others that you should live together quite happily.

There is, however, one great obstacle that could spoil everything. Your Libra man loves luxury and comfort and you want the clothes to match the environment. Unfortunately, neither of you has much inclination to work for these things. Money management could always be a problem for you two. If you can give each other the moral support to say 'No, we cannot afford it,' you may be able to keep out of financial trouble.

Both Libra and Pisces people possess a well-developed aesthetic sense, which should result in your home being the admiration of all your friends. You are able to create interior designs that are outstanding without being prohibitively expensive. You may be a couple, in fact, who could earn your living in this or a similar field of the decorative arts.

A Libra-Pisces relationship may always be at risk because you both find it difficult to say no and people may try to impose on your good nature. This is another case when you should give each other moral support to protect your own interests.

Your love life should be everything any couple could wish for. You are both very loving, very understanding and constantly aware of each other's needs. Not many people experience your kind of physical relationship.

This could be a marvellous marriage if you can learn to run your domestic and financial affairs with some degree of efficiency.

CHARTS

MARRIAGE COMPATIBILITY

Man	Woman
Libra	Aries
Libra	Taurus
Libra	Gemini

Marriage compatibility	Nature
Fairly good	Libra's lack of ambition could be frustrating for Aries, but with care she can persuade him to make more effort.
Fairly good	Both are interested in a home as a place of comfort and good taste, but Libra may need to make more effort on behalf of this partnership.
Some difficulty	Success in this partnership depends very much on both partners making a joint effort to secure stability.

Man	Woman
Libra	Cancer
Libra	Leo
Libra	Virgo
Libra	Libra

Marriage compatibility	Nature
Fairly good	Lack of leadership is the main threat to an otherwise potentially successful partnership. Cancer's need for security and Libra's willingness to please could be the solution.
Fairly good	Sensible management of domestic and financial affairs will eliminate any threat to a successful partnership.
Some difficulty	Virgo's preoccupation with hard work and efficiency could make Libra miserable. All could be well if she learns to relax and enjoy her Libra man's company.
Fairly good	Two very easy-going people. If finances are well-managed and both make a fair contribution to their joint responsibilities, a successful partnership is assured.

Man	Woman
Libra	Scorpio
Libra	Sagittarius
Libra	Capricorn

Marriage compatibility	Nature
Some difficulty	Strong-willed and jealous Scorpio can make or break this partnership. If Libra makes a real effort to meet Scorpio's ambitions, and mutual trust is established, all will be well.
Fairly good	Finances may always be a problem. Libra's willingness to give Sagittarius time to acquire knowledge should be appreciated by her making Libra a comfortable home.
Some difficulty	Capricorn woman can mould easy-going Libra to help her achieve her long-term ambitions. Libra is always willing to cooperate, but Capricorn can impose on his good nature.

Man	Woman
Libra	Aquarius
Libra	Pisces

Marriage compatibility	Nature
Fairly good	A marriage of minds that can succeed because both partners have the ability to communicate long after most couples have nothing left to say to each other.
Fairly good	A Libra-Pisces partnership is always at risk because they are loath to forego pleasures they cannot always afford.

THE MOST
TOLERANT HUSBANDS

Aries   Perhaps the most intolerant of all the signs,
               tends to please himself with little regard
               for the feelings of others.

Taurus   Is easy-going, but has very strong views
               on everything, including his wife's role in
               marriage. Not the man for women who
               need a degree of freedom.

Gemini   A very tolerant man, mainly because he
               has so many interests that he has little time
               to think about you or what you are doing.

Cancer   This man is very possessive and his peace
               of mind depends to a large extent on your
               constant companionship.

Leo   Leo man is a freedom-lover, but is unlikely
               to deny you the same degree of freedom he
               expects to have.

Virgo   Your Virgo man is very critical, and con-
               scious of what society thinks of him and
               his wife. Not a man to encourage you to do
               your own thing.

Libra   This man is loath to make an issue out
               of anything. Peace-at-any-price is his
               motto and he is unlikely to oppose your
               desire for a degree of freedom.

Scorpio   A Scorpio man is jealous and suspicious. If you are one of the freedom-loving types, you may have difficulty with this man.

Sagittarius   Believes in 'live and let live' and is very unlikely to restrict your desire to have some time to yourself.

Capricorn   A pillar of society who can be too concerned about what other people think, with the result that he will not encourage you to have interests outside the home.

Aquarius   A freedom-lover and the most tolerant of husbands. He is very willing for you to have a life of your own, and may even encourage it.

Pisces   There are two types: one can't bear to be away from you, and the other is content to dream his dreams while you are left to your own devices.

YOUR MAN'S AFFECTIONS

SUN SIGN

Aries   An Aries man is impetuous, easily aroused and flirtatious.

Taurus   Your Taurus man has very strong affections, but quite often hides his real emotions.

Gemini   A Gemini man's affections are lightweight and he rarely gets deeply involved. He is notorious for having more than one woman.

Cancer	Cancer man loves with his heart and soul, and can be very possessive.
Leo	Leo man gives his love and affection unreservedly. His heart will always rule his head.
Virgo	A Virgo man has very firm control of his affections, and is usually a very devoted husband.
Libra	Your Libra man is tenderly affectionate and very susceptible to the attention other women give him.
Scorpio	The most passionate and demanding man, often very possessive and jealous.
Sagittarius	This man's affections are sincere, but he is often too shy to express his love for you.
Capricorn	A Capricorn man is quietly sincere, but he is also often too shy to express his love for you.
Aquarius	This man's affections are lightweight. He prefers his relationships to remain on a mental, rather than a physical, plane.
Pisces	A Pisces man not only loves, he worships his women.

If you would like further advice for yourself or your man, write directly to the author at the address below. Be sure to include the time, date and place of birth of the person concerned. *Please enclose stamps or a stamped, self-addressed envelope* for reply.

J. S. Gunn
P.O. Box 2
167A Newgate Street
Bishop Auckland
County Durham
DL14 7EN
England

MILLS & BOON ASTRAL GUIDES

YOU AND YOUR ARIES MAN
YOU AND YOUR TAURUS MAN
YOU AND YOUR GEMINI MAN
YOU AND YOUR CANCER MAN
YOU AND YOUR LEO MAN
YOU AND YOUR VIRGO MAN
YOU AND YOUR LIBRA MAN
YOU AND YOUR SCORPIO MAN
YOU AND YOUR SAGITTARIUS MAN
YOU AND YOUR CAPRICORN MAN
YOU AND YOUR AQUARIUS MAN
YOU AND YOUR PISCES MAN

FIESTA SERIES !

ALL PRICED AT 20p. SEE OVER FOR HANDY ORDER FORM. PLEASE TICK YOUR REQUIREMENTS.